*Laughter is the
closest thing to
the grace of God.*

Karl Barth

101 ways to enjoy God

Candy Paull

SPIRIT PRESS

101 Ways to Enjoy God
ISBN: 1-40372-012-6

Published in 2006 by Spirit Press, an imprint of Dalmatian Press, LLC.
Copyright © 2006 Dalmatian Press, LLC. Franklin, Tennessee 37067.

Editor: Lila Empson
Text Designer: Whisner Design Group

06 07 08 09 QSR 10 9 8 7 6 5 4 3 2 1

Printed in Canada

14930

Look at everything as though you were seeing it for the first time or the last time. Then your time on earth will be filled with glory.

Betty Smith

Contents

Contents continued...

Introduction

Have you taken a moment to enjoy God lately? This little book has been created to help you do just that. You might light a candle and spend a few moments in prayer. Or you could go for a walk in the woods and meditate on the beauty of God's creation. You can read the Bible or sing songs of praise. You can enjoy God by sharing his love with others and serving the needs of the community. From introspective moments alone with God to joyous worship with other believers, this book offers simple suggestions to help you celebrate your relationship with God.

May the love and grace of Christ rule in your heart today. May this little book help you enjoy God every day.

The person you are now, the person you have been, the person you will be — this person God has chosen as beloved.

William Countryman

*The fundamental fact
of existence is that this
trust in God, this faith, is
the firm foundation under
everything that makes life
worth living. It's our handle
on what we can't see.*

Hebrews 11:1
THE MESSAGE

God is in the details.

Mies van der Rohe

#1

Cultivate a Grateful Heart

It's easy to focus on the things you want and what you don't have. Instead of encouraging the weeds of dissatisfaction in your spiritual garden, cultivate a grateful heart instead.

A grateful heart gives you the insight to see small beauties and gentle gifts from the hand of God. The smile on the face of a loved one, the laughter of friends, a chorus of birds at dawn, the common blessings of milk and cereal and coffee and eggs—all these are simple gifts to be grateful for. Enjoy life and enjoy God by thanking him for all the wonderful gifts he brings to you today.

grateful

I will tell everyone of your justice and goodness, and I will praise you all day long.
Psalm 35:28 NLT

>> Make a list of twenty-five things you are grateful for.

#2

Lift Your Hands in Praise

> *I will honor you as long as I live, lifting up my hands to you in prayer.*
> Psalm 63:4 NLT

praise

You praise God with your body as well as your mind. One beautiful and biblical way to praise is to lift your hands. Let your hands reach up to heaven, as a child raises her hands to be lifted by a loving parent. As you praise and worship God, dedicate your hands to be used for his highest purposes.

The hands symbolize not only the work you do, but the way you receive. Praise God for all the gifts you have received from his hands. As you lift your hands to heaven, open yourself to receive the blessings God wants to shower upon you.

>> The next time you pray, lift both hands to God and give praise for who he is and the gifts he gives you.

#3

Practice the Presence of God

A monk who lived in the fifteenth century wrote a classic book about practicing the presence of God in daily life. Brother Lawrence meditated silently in his heart on God's love, even as he washed the monastery pots and pans. He wrote, "I worshiped God as often as I could, keeping my mind in his holy presence."

Over the centuries, his little book has inspired men and women to pray and meditate in the midst of their daily tasks. Practicing the presence of God reminds you that everything you do has meaning and purpose when done with prayer and dedication.

> *Rejoice always, pray without ceasing, in everything give thanks; for this is the will of God in Christ Jesus for you.*
> 1 Thessalonians 5:16–18 NKJV

>> The next time you wash dishes, do laundry, mow the lawn, or sweep the floor, practice the presence of God and meditate on his greatness.

#4

Create Something Beautiful for God

> *Truth exists for the wise, beauty for the feeling heart.*
>
> Johann von Schiller

create

God created you in his image. Your creativity is a gift from God, and the way you use your creativity is your gift back to God. Home crafts, fine art, beautiful music, useful objects that are well designed and well made are all expressions of the creative spirit.

Whatever you make, create it for God's glory as well as humanity's use. It can be as simple as an arrangement of flowers for your table, or as complex as an exquisitely crafted piece of furniture. Whatever you create, make it something that satisfies your heart, takes your best effort, and becomes a worthy offering to God.

>> Start a project that satisfies your desire for beauty and finish it. Display it or use it in your home.

#5

Serve Someone in Need

Look around and you'll see that there are many opportunities to serve others. God created people to share with one another. Being able to give to someone in need is as great a blessing as being given what you need.

Extend your hand in generous service. There are wonderful organizations, like Habitat for Humanity, that use volunteer service to help others help themselves. Your church or local charity can use an extra pair of hands and a loving heart. Your next-door neighbor may need a helping hand or an encouraging word. When you share yourself with others, you'll be sharing yourself with God.

serve

You will find, as you look back upon your life, that the moments that stand out are the moments when you have done things for others.
Henry Drummond

>> Say "I'd love to" when someone makes a request. Volunteer at a church or a charity.

Step Out in Faith

> *The LORD is on my side; I will not fear. What can man do to me?*
> Psalm 118:6 NKJV

faith

You've been hesitating, wondering if you should or you shouldn't, teetering on the edge of a pool, trying to decide whether to dive in or not. You waver on the edge of a decision. You've weighed the pros and cons, prayed about what to do next. Now it's time to take that first step.

Go ahead. Step out in faith. God is with you and will walk with you every step of the way. Even if you make mistakes, those mistakes will serve a higher purpose. Remember, no one can steer a parked car. So get moving and see where God steers you.

>> Ask God to guide you before you decide. Make a decision and see where it takes you.

#7

Spend Time in Spiritual Reading

The Bible offers the ultimate in spiritual reading, but it can be supplemented with other kinds of reading as well. In his book on spiritual reading, *Take and Read*, pastor and writer Eugene Peterson observed, "Spiritual reading does not mean reading on spiritual or religious subjects, but reading any book that comes to hand in a spiritual way, which is to say, listening to the Spirit, alert to intimations of God."

Start with the Psalms. Then move into spiritual classics and books about the spiritual life. Remember that good novels, poetry, and history can feed your spirit as well as feed your mind.

r e a d i n g

> *Spiritual reading is mostly a lover's activity—a dalliance with words, reading as much between the lines as in the lines themselves.*
> Eugene Peterson

>> Pick a good book to be your companion for daily spiritual reading.

#8

Practice a Simple Heart Meditation

> *Blessed are the pure in heart, for they shall see God.*
> Matthew 5:8 NKJV

meditate

Here is a simple meditation technique that can remind you to listen to your heart and hear what God wants to say to you. You can do it in the middle of a busy day. This simple, unobtrusive action will remind you to stay connected to your spirit.

Find a quiet place to be alone. Close your eyes, bow your head, and put both hands over your heart. Now breathe deeply. Focus your thoughts and become aware that God is with you, as close as your beating heart. Ask for guidance and thank God for your blessings. Now open your eyes and go on with your day.

>> Make a decision to surrender to God and commit to living your life fully, with your whole heart.

#9

Sing with Your Whole Heart

You don't have to be a great singer to sing from the heart. All you have to do is have the heart to sing, and be willing to sing in spite of your fears or objections. Singing is a wonderful antidote to depression. It's a great faith lifter, as well. If you're shy about singing, you can start by singing at home. Sing hymns around the house, happy songs in the shower, and choruses in the car.

Join in the hymns and praise songs at church. Consider becoming a part of the choir. Be brave and sing, making melody in your heart to God.

Unbutton my lips, dear God; I'll let loose with your praise.
Psalm 51:15
THE MESSAGE

>> Enjoy singing hymns and songs of praise in church. Sing in the shower or while you do chores around the house.

#10

Dress Up and Go to Church

> *Worship the
> LORD in the beauty
> of holiness!*
>
> 1 Chronicles 16:29
> NKJV

church

Make church a special occasion. Instead of saving the elegant hats and the well-cut suits for only Easter and funerals, make this Sunday a celebration. It's wonderful to wear comfortable, casual clothes, as people are doing in churches nowadays. But every once in a while, it's a good thing to be reminded that going to the house of God is a special occasion.

So dress in your best clothes. Put that lovely crown of a hat on your beautiful head. Polish your shoes and wear your brightest smile. Let your outer beauty reflect your inner beauty as you go and worship God.

>> Buy or make a festive outfit to wear to worship services.

#11

Make Time for Silence

It's a noisy world out there. Car alarms, sirens, elevator music, traffic, stereos, television, radio, and a cacophony of other sounds assault your ears daily. Even when you get home, the noise of televisions, lawn mowers, and household appliances can drown out the quiet.

silence

Take a breather from all that noise. Find a quiet place to settle your spirit—whether it is a corner of your house, the interior of a cathedral or other place of worship, or out in the great outdoors. Slow down and listen. Some secrets can only be whispered, not spoken. Let God whisper to you in the silence.

> *Be still, and know that I am God.*
> Psalm 46:10 NKJV

>> Make an appointment with yourself to spend time in silence and prayer. Choose a quiet place to be alone with God.

#12

Read the Good Book

> The Bible is not only a book which I can understand, it is a book which understands me.
>
> Emile Caillet

read

It's been a bestseller for centuries, beloved by men and women across cultures and through time. The Bible is a collection of sixty-six books written over the span of six thousand years. It's a treasure chest of wisdom, poetry, history, parable, biography, and prophecy.

Make Bible reading a regular part of your day. A few minutes of reading in the morning can set the tone for the rest of the day. Meditate on what you read and let it speak to your heart. You will discover help, guidance, and insight for living in the pages of this God-breathed book.

>> Read a chapter a day in the Bible. Or buy a one-year Bible that divides the Scriptures into daily readings.

#13

Meet God in the Wilderness

Jesus went away to the wilderness and desert to meet with his heavenly Father. Follow his example and go out to the wild places to meet with God. Whether it is by a roaring ocean, a quiet lake, a grand canyon, a desert rock, a field of wildflowers, or an ancient forest, the wilderness reminds you of the Creator's greatness.

Take a few moments to be still before God. As sunlight filters through a canopy of tall trees, sit on a stone and contemplate the wonder of creation. It is so beautiful that you can't help but worship the God who made it all.

meet

You will find something more in woods than in books. Trees and stones will teach you what you cannot learn from masters.

Saint Bernard of Clairvaux

>> Take a walk away in some beautiful wild place and set aside part of that time to be still and worship God in the wilderness.

#14

Light a Candle

Everything exposed by the light becomes visible, for it is light that makes everything visible.

Ephesians 5:13–14
NIV

light

A taper is lit and brings light into the sanctuary. You're used to the idea of candles for church services or for romantic dinners. But consider using the lighting of a candle to create sacred space and mark out sacred time in your day.

Choose a candle and a candle-holder especially for this purpose. When you light the candle during your prayer and devotional time, let its flickering flame remind you that you are setting that particular time and space apart for God. Meditate on the quality of light and how God illuminates your life with his light.

>> Choose a special candle to use for your quiet time with God. Let it mark the hours you spend in prayer.

#15

Be Open to Unexpected Gifts from God

gifts

Your daily calendar tells you that everything is scheduled and accounted for—but your calendar cannot predict the unexpected. Even the most mundane days can hold surprises and gifts from the hand of God, if you are receptive to them.

You thought you were only running errands, but you ran into an old friend in line at the bank. It was just another ordinary day until that glorious sunset took your breath away. The sun shining through parted clouds chased away the gloom of rain. A smile, a red rose, an unexpected encounter—God loves to surprise his children every single day.

> *Look at everything as though you were seeing it for the first time or the last time. Then your time on earth will be filled with glory.*
>
> Betty Smith

>> Surprise someone you love with an unexpected gift—flowers, a card, chocolate—something simple to celebrate life together.

cultivate

101 ways to

praise

meditate

create

serve

enjoy God

step out

sing

dress up

#16
Pray the Psalms

> *I meditate on your age-old laws; O LORD, they comfort me.*
>
> Psalm 119:52 NLT

pray

Christians have been praying the psalms for centuries, both corporately and individually. Nothing in Scripture or tradition has shaped the prayers of God's people as the book of Psalms.

Praying a psalm is not the same as studying a psalm. Praying is done in the context of a loving personal relationship, while studying seeks knowledge and understanding. Choose a psalm and make it your personal prayer. Or follow the tradition of reading through all of the psalms on a regular basis. *The Book of Common Prayer* divides the psalms into thirty-day readings and offers a format used by believers around the world.

>> Choose a meaningful psalm (for example, Psalm 23, Psalm 139, or Psalm 42) and make it your personal prayer.

#17

Plant a Seed Prayer

A tiny black seed holds the potential for leaves, flowers, and fruition when it's planted in rich soil, watered, and cultivated. A simple prayer holds the same creative power when you plant it in the soil of faith and tend it with love.

When you have a mountain to move, start by planting a seed prayer. It doesn't have to be complicated. Make your request known to God. Then thank God that the answer is coming, even though you may not yet know how. Make a marker in your garden of faith and then give it time to grow in God's grace.

plant

> *I tell you the truth, if you have faith as small as a mustard seed, you can say to this mountain, "Move from here to there" and it will move. Nothing will be impossible for you.*
>
> Matthew 17:20–21
> NIV

>> Create a prayer journal where you can keep track of prayer requests and prayers answered.

#18

See the Sacred in the Ordinary

Since everything God created is good, we should not reject any of it. We may receive it gladly, with thankful hearts.

1 Timothy 4:4 NLT

sacred

All of life can be an experience of the sacred, if you have the eyes to see. The ordinary things you take for granted can be metaphors of God's love and reminders of God's presence in your life.

Look for the sacred in the ordinary details of everyday life. The simple act of cooking a meal can be an offering of love. Washing dishes reminds you of spiritual cleansing. The sun on your face feels like a benediction. Conversing with a friend or loved one offers a counterpoint to your conversations with God. Look at "ordinary" things as extraordinary gifts from the hand of God.

>> Take one mundane task you do regularly, such as cooking meals, and meditate on it as a metaphor for what God is doing in your life.

#19

Memorize Inspirational Words

Sometimes you need an encouraging word when life gets difficult. One way to cheer yourself on is to find and memorize inspirational and encouraging words. A great quote, a Bible promise, a poem, a section of Scripture—these make great companions when the road seems long and rocky.

Search out inspirational words or Scriptures that are meaningful to you. Then learn them by heart. You'll be surprised at how often those words will pop into your mind just when you need them the most. Memorization plants seeds of inspiration in your mind that grow to full fruition in your heart and in your life.

memorize

> *If you don't know what you're doing, pray to the Father. He loves to help. You'll get his help, and won't be condescended to when you ask for it.*
>
> James 1:5
> THE MESSAGE

>> Memorize a comforting Bible verse (such as Romans 8:28) or a section of Scripture (such as Psalm 23).

#20

Write an Inspirational Poem or Song

> *Sing hymns instead of drinking songs! Sing songs from your heart to Christ.*
>
> Ephesians 5:19
> THE MESSAGE

write

Sometimes it's important to say something in your own words, in your own way. No one can say it quite like you—and God is listening eagerly to what you have to share.

Nurture your creative heart by writing a poem of praise. Sing your love to God with a song you wrote just for him. You don't have to be a published author or professional songwriter to delight in the gifts of word and song. God gave you a mind and a voice, and he loves to see you use them. Offer your creative gift to God and see how he blesses it.

>> Take a blank piece of paper and write a brief poem to God about something you saw or did today.

#21

Go On a Spiritual Retreat

Sometimes it takes a time away from your regular round to recharge your spiritual batteries. Take a spiritual retreat away from home.

Choose something that suits your personality and spiritual practice. It could be a silent retreat weekend at a monastery, a camp revival week with singing and baptisms, a church gathering at a local campground, an intense immersion in prayer and Bible study, or a friendly gathering of like-minded spiritual seekers. Many church camps and retreat centers offer a variety of options to suit your needs. Ask for God's guidance. He will lead you to the right retreat for you.

retreat

In returning and rest you shall be saved; in quietness and confidence shall be your strength.

Isaiah 30:15 NKJV

>> Research retreat centers in your area or in a part of the country you would like to visit.

#22

Cultivate a Christlike Spirit

> *Let this mind be in you which was also in Christ Jesus.*
>
> Philippians 2:5 NKJV

spirit

You have it in you to be like Christ, both in character and in your relationships with others. As he loved, so you also can choose to love. As he forgave, so you also can choose to forgive. As he stood for truth no matter what the cost, so you also can choose to stand for truth in your corner of the world.

Today, ask yourself, "What would Jesus do?" What would Jesus do if he met your angry neighbor? How would Jesus react to the driver who cut you off in traffic? Would Jesus care about being with the "right" people? Whom would Jesus reach out to help?

>> Read about and meditate on the life of Christ. The Gospel of John is an excellent place to start.

#23

Celebrate the Seasons of the Church Year

The church year offers a rich resource for Christian celebration and contemplation. Liturgies and Scripture readings create a devotional framework for services and personal devotions. Following the seasons of the year and the festivals of the church helps you remember the life of Christ.

In winter, Advent, Christmas, and Epiphany celebrate the entry of Christ into the world and the revelation of his light. Lent and Easter take you through his death and resurrection, into spring renewal. Pentecost commemorates the birth of the church, while Ordinary Time takes you through summer and into autumn's harvest bounty.

celebrate

> *Liturgical time is essentially poetic time, oriented toward process rather than productivity, willing to wait attentively in stillness rather than always pushing to "get the job done."*
>
> Kathleen Norris

>> Look through *The Book of Common Prayer*, a guide through the church year that has been used by believers for centuries.

#24

Give a Special Offering

> *The world of the generous gets larger and larger; the world of the stingy gets smaller and smaller.*
>
> Proverbs 11:24
> THE MESSAGE

give

When you are feeling a bit worried about finances, or if a personal concern is weighing on your mind, consider giving a special offering. Giving is an act of faith. Give cheerfully and willingly, for God rewards a generous heart in his own time and in his own way.

Whether you want to celebrate good news or happy events with a thank offering, or make a statement of faith that God can meet all of your needs in tight times as well as good times, a special offering over and above your usual giving can be a powerful statement of faith.

>> Give an anonymous offering to your church, a favorite charity, or to someone in need.

#25

Pray with a Friend

One of the most encouraging things you can do is to meet regularly with a friend for prayer. Having a prayer partner can be a life-changing experience. It can transform your prayer life.

It's easier to stay constant in prayer when you know you're going to be seeing your prayer partner that week. Keep track of prayer requests and answers. Keep the format for prayer time simple and positive. Discuss your concerns and pray for each other, but also make time to pray for others, for the issues and problems of the day, and for the work of God in the world.

pray

If two of you agree on earth concerning anything that they ask, it will be done for them by My Father in heaven.

Matthew 18:19
NKJV

>> Commit to a prayer partnership with a friend. Get together regularly and pray for each other every day.

#26
Spend Time with God Daily

If you look for me in earnest, you will find me when you seek me.

Jeremiah 29:13 NLT

time

If you want to cultivate a friendship, you need to spend time together on a regular basis. It's the same when you want to cultivate your relationship with God. A daily quiet time can be your appointment to talk over the issues of your life with the God who cares for you.

Create a sense of intimacy by lighting a candle. Meet at the same time every day, when possible. Make yourself comfortable to meet with your Friend. You might want to read Scriptures or a devotional book. This is your time alone with God, so make it special and unique to you.

>> Set aside a regular time for daily prayer and meditation. Put it in your schedule.

#27

Write a Letter to God

God is as close as your breath, as intimate as your heartbeat. He is always with you and will never forsake you. However, since you cannot see God, sometimes it is difficult to imagine his reality in your life. One simple way to be closer to God is to write a letter, as if you are writing to a dear friend who loves you and who is concerned about what is happening in your life.

Since no one but you and God will see this letter, hold nothing back. Tell him about your struggles and triumphs. Close it with love and sign your name.

write

> *A letter shows the man it is written to as well as the man it is written by.*
>
> Lord Chesterfield

>> Write a letter to God about what you are experiencing today. Write it as if you're writing a long, loving letter to a concerned friend.

#28

Create Sacred Space

> *Holy, holy, holy is the LORD Almighty; the whole earth is full of his glory.*
>
> Isaiah 6:3 NIV

create

God is everywhere, even in the midst of your cluttered den or cozy kitchen. But sometimes it helps to set aside a sacred space where you can go to meet God. Set aside a quiet nook, a special room, or a small tabletop for times of personal worship and meditation.

You might want to keep a Bible to read, a prayer book, pictures of loved ones, and other meaningful things in this place. Fresh flowers and beautiful objects can be reminders that this place is set apart from daily business. Lighting a candle can also mark this place as a sacred time to meet with God.

>> Create a sacred space anywhere by sanctifying it with a simple prayer of consecration, knowing that God meets you wherever you are.

#29

Share in the Laughter of Creation

A puppy chases its tail with youthful enthusiasm. Monkeys chatter in trees at your local zoo. Children laugh with glee as they swing higher and higher on the swing set at the park. Teenage girls giggle at a slumber party. The spring sun shines on budding flowers and new leaves, so that even the very earth seems to be filled with green laughter.

Life, especially when it's feeling young and new, is filled with the genesis laughter of creation. Share in this laughter by looking at the lighter side of life and seeing a world filled with God's creativity and splendor.

share

> *Laughter is the closest thing to the grace of God.*
> Karl Barth

>> Watch children and puppies play, and think about the grace of God that has been demonstrated so freely in a laughing, lovely creation.

#30

Listen to Music

Music is for the soul what wind is for the ship, blowing her onwards in the direction in which she is steered.

William Booth

listen

The soaring harmonies of Gregorian chant echo against the stone ribs of a Gothic cathedral. The elegant intricacies of Bach roll out of a great organ. "Ode to Joy" brings Beethoven's Ninth Symphony to a grand finale. A gospel choir swings with a contagious rhythm. Great hymns of the church fill the sanctuary. A simple voice and guitar lead the group in a praise chorus.

Music is one of the most powerful ways to lift your spirits. Listening to music, as well as singing, can usher you into the presence of God. Let music prepare you for worship and fill your heart with joy and praise.

>> Buy some recorded music that can be used for personal worship, praise, and meditation.

#31
Pay Attention

attention

Paying attention seems simple. You think you're doing it when you listen to a friend telling you about his or her day, but how often does your mind wander to what's next on your list of things to do? Paying attention means keeping your mind in the moment, taking in what's really happening, what's really being said, instead of some mental scenario about the future or past.

When you practice paying attention, you learn more about your friend. You can use this skill in your relationship with God, too. Paying attention helps you delight in his presence because your focus is on being with him.

> *Post this at all the intersections, dear friends: Lead with your ears, follow up with your tongue, and let anger straggle along in the rear.*
>
> James 1:19
> THE MESSAGE

>> The next time you talk to someone, give them your full attention. The next time you pray, pay full attention to God.

pray

101 ways to

plant

experiene

memorize

nurture

enjoy God

retreat

celebrate

give

#32

Write in Your Journal

> *Be earnest and disciplined in your prayers.*
>
> 1 Peter 4:7 NLT

write

Not everyone keeps a journal. But it is a tried-and-true tool that has helped many people cultivate a deeper spiritual life. If you have never explored the art of journaling, think about trying it.

You can create a journal that fits your needs. A prayer journal keeps track of prayers, answers, and insights on prayer. A daily journal offers space for writing thoughts, insights, and feelings, helping you get clear on what is most important to you. You can share your thoughts with God by writing them out. Writing in a journal is an active form of meditation that can help you cultivate a richer relationship with God.

>> Purchase a beautiful blank journal. Or make a simple journal out of a school notebook and decorate the cover yourself.

#33

Discover God Through Beauty

The world is full of beauty, if you have eyes to see. The world is filled with God's glory for those who know where to look. Beauty in nature and beauty created by human hands both reflect God's grace. The faces of the people you love can be the most beautiful reflection of God's love in your life.

Learning to see God's hand in the beauty around you helps you draw closer to him. From the beauty of a stained-glass window to the splendor of a crimson sunset, beauty can lead you to contemplate the greatness and glory of the God who created all beauty.

beauty

Beauty is God's handwriting. Welcome it in every fair face, every fair day, every fair flower.

Charles Kingsley

>> Buy or make something you think is beautiful for your home: a rose-bush for your garden or a well-made piece of furniture for your living room.

#34
Simplify Your Life

> *Finding a way to live the simple life today is man's most complicated task.*
>
> Henry A. Courtney

simplify

Simplicity is a spiritual virtue. When your schedule is too full, your house is cluttered, and you feel overwhelmed by the demands of daily life, take steps to simplify. If you are distracted by too much to do and too many things, you won't have energy for your relationship with God.

Make room for God to do a new thing in your life by clearing away old things. If what you own seems to own you, release that which no longer serves you. Don't let clutter accumulate. Simplify your life so you can cultivate your spiritual life.

>> Eliminate the activities, relationships, and things that drain you to make room for those that are more authentic and supportive.

#35

Take a Day Away

It's a bright sunny day, and the great outdoors is calling to you. You've been busy and productive, working through your list of things to do. Now you need to escape and take a day away. And when you leave home, take a pocket Bible with you so you can spend part of that day enjoying being away alone with God.

Take a walk and find a quiet place to contemplate the scene before you. There is something very powerful about reading the Scriptures and praying in a wild or beautiful place. It's a wonderful reminder that God is with you wherever you go.

take

The earth shall be full of the knowledge of the LORD as the waters cover the sea.

Isaiah 11:9 NKJV

>> Mark your calendar to take a day off. Take a picnic lunch and a Bible, and make time to read, meditate, and pray during your time away.

#36

Join the Choir

> *I wept at the beauty of your hymns and canticles, and was powerfully moved at the sweet sound of your Church singing. These sounds flowed into my ears, and the truth streamed into my heart.*
>
> Saint Augustine

choir

Join together with others and sing praises to God. Some of the most beautiful music ever composed has been written for worship. Singing in harmony with others will lift your spirits and create moments of beauty and praise for others.

If you don't already sing in a choir, consider joining one. Most volunteer choirs welcome new members and want people to join in. Or you can gather some friends together to sing hymns, inspirational songs, or carols for people in nursing homes and hospitals. Joining with others in song lifts your spirits and makes worshiping God more meaningful and enjoyable.

>> Find a church or community choir you can join. Enjoy singing with others.

#37

Live in the Moment

God is speaking to you in the midst of each moment. No matter how mundane or commonplace, a hidden holiness lies beneath the surface of your life. When you focus on the past or the future, you miss the moment that is right in front of you and miss the message that God wants to speak to you here and now.

Live fully and attentively right now. See this as a holy moment, a time of communion with God. Sense the sweetness of the day. Know life for the miracle that it is and savor each moment as a gift from God.

live

Receive every day as a resurrection from death, as a new enjoyment of life.

William Law

>> Take a moment to be still. Observe the sights, sounds, scents, and sensations that surround you. Be awake to the miracle of your life.

#38

See Your Life as a Sacred Journey

> *I think of my life and the lives of everyone who has ever lived, or will ever live, not just as journeys through time, but as sacred journeys.*
>
> Frederick Buechner

journey

"By faith Abraham, when called to go to a place he would later receive as his inheritance, obeyed and went, even though he did not know where he was going" (Hebrews 11:8 NIV). You are like Abraham. You step out into life and do not know where it will take you. Yet you can look back and see how God led you step by step.

See your life as a sacred journey, traveled by faith. Childhood, marriage, parenthood, celebrations, sorrows—all are milestones marking your sacred journey through life. Like Abraham, you are following God's call to a promised land you have never seen.

>> Think of your life as a map, marked by the milestones along the way. Determine where you are on your sacred journey.

#39

Taste and See That the Lord Is Good

What does it mean to "taste and see that the Lord is good"? God is not a chocolate dessert or a delicious dinner you can eat. It is spiritual hunger that he feeds. God's goodness nourishes the soul. When you spend time in the awareness of God's presence, each moment contains a sweetness that feeds the spirit, satisfying your heart in deep and mysterious ways.

When life loses its savor, go away to a quiet place and let God refresh you. Just being in God's presence is enough to satisfy that hunger and thirst for righteousness—filling your spirit with his holy sweetness.

taste

Taste and see that the LORD is good. Oh, the joys of those who trust in him!

Psalm 34:8 NLT

>> For a more literal experience of tasting God, go to a Communion service and share in the bread and wine.

#40

Acknowledge the Help You Have Received

> *I cried out to the LORD in my suffering, and he heard me. He set me free from all my fears.*
>
> Psalm 34:6 NLT

help

When times are tough and you're not sure how you're going to get through them, take a minute to acknowledge the help you have received. Parents, pastors, teachers, friends, mentors—you've been helped by many people.

Remember the blessings and thank those who have helped you in the past. Honor them for the gifts they have given you: a helping hand, an encouraging word, a stirring example. Focus on the help you've received instead of the needs you still have. When you look back at how God has provided for you, it will inspire you to believe that God will provide for you again.

>> Send a thank-you note to someone who helped or encouraged you.

#41

Say Grace Before Meals

It's an old-fashioned picture. Heads are bowed, hands are folded, and the family says grace before they begin passing the plates. But saying grace is more than just an activity for old-fashioned families at Thanksgiving feasts. Saying grace is an old-fashioned habit that modern people can make part of their own lives.

Make saying grace a part of your life. A simple bowing of the head and a "thank you for this food" will suffice. Whether you dine alone with cornflakes and milk or feast with friends and family, saying grace is another way to become aware of God's presence and provision.

g r a c e

> *Gratitude to God makes even a temporal blessing a taste of heaven.*
>
> William Romaine

>> The next time you sit down to dinner, thank God for your food before you eat.

#42

Explore Theology

> *To be a theologian is to pray truly and to pray truly is to be a theologian.*
>
> Evagrius

theology

When you think of reading theology, do you think of hefting some brick of a book more suited to being a doorstop than reading material? Though there are theological books that fit that description, and books that depict theologians trying to figure out how many angels can dance on the head of a pin, theology books can open mental doors.

But theology isn't just about head knowledge. Theology can help you understand and enjoy God more. The best theology speaks to the heart as well as the mind. If you are intrigued by what others have to say about God, explore some theology.

>> Just for the fun of it, check out the theology section of your local bookstore or library.

#43

Resolve to Be a Blessing to Others

Make a conscious choice today that you will be a blessing to others. As God has blessed you, so pass that blessing on to the world around you. How can you be a blessing? You can bless others with an encouraging word or helping hand. You can also be a silent blessing, sending prayers of blessing to everyone you encounter, whether you speak to them or not. God wants to bless the world through you, and because you're here, you can trust he has a purpose for your life. Ask God to guide you and he will make you a blessing to the world.

blessing

> *Blessed is he who has regard for the weak; the LORD delivers him in times of trouble.*
>
> Psalm 41:1 NIV

>> For one day, say a silent prayer of blessing for each person you encounter.

#44

Look for Good in Every Situation

> *Surely goodness and love will follow me all the days of my life, and I will dwell in the house of the LORD forever.*
>
> Psalm 23:6 NIV

good

Look for the good (and God) in every situation. God is always present, even in those times when he seems far away. Though troubles may veil his presence the way clouds hide the sun, he is still there.

It takes an act of radical faith to look for light in the midst of darkness. This faith grows out of a decision to trust God even when you cannot see. By looking for the good, you become more sensitive to the hidden ways of God. It may be awhile before you understand, but God will reveal his presence and goodness to you.

>> Think about a difficult situation you are facing. How might God's goodness be hiding within your troubles?

#45

Plant Hope in Your Heart

At a baby blessing, the expectant parents asked friends to help them plant an oak tree in honor of their coming son. They were planting the dream of the boy growing along with the tree, and the tree represented the hope that the child would grow sturdy and strong, deeply rooted in love.

In the same way, you can plant a seed of hope in your heart for dreams yet to be born. Cultivate that seed by taking steps to make your dreams reality. Water it with prayer. Make God a partner in your dreaming and enjoy the process of making dreams come to fruition with him.

hope

Faith is being sure of what we hope for and certain of what we do not see.

Hebrews 11:1 NIV

>> Plant a seed in a pot and watch it grow—or, if you have plenty of space and a big dream, plant a tree as a symbol of your hope.

#46

Create an Affirmation

I used to ask God to help me. Then I asked if I might help Him. I ended up by asking Him to do His work through me.

James Hudson Taylor

create

Affirmative prayer helps you enjoy a positive prayer relationship with God. You become a creative partner with God. Speak positive words about yourself and your situation in the present tense, affirming that these things are true and that you trust God to make them true in your life. Write out your personal affirmation and post it in a prominent place.

You can also take a favorite Bible promise and turn it into a personal affirmation. Affirmations are faith-builders that encourage your heart.

>> Turn a Scripture verse into a personal affirmation; for example: The peace of God rules in my heart (Colossians 3:15).

#47

Meditate on a Section of Scripture

One way to nourish your spirit is to take a psalm or a section of Scripture and meditate on it over a period of time. As you live with the words, they will take root in your heart and mind, revealing new facets of meaning as time goes by. The words will become the living Word to you rather than just words on the page.

For instance, meditating on the section of the Gospel of John where Jesus compares himself to the vine and his followers to the branches (John 15:1–17) becomes even more meaningful when you watch spring come to the garden.

meditate

Meditation is the devotional practice of pondering the words of a verse, or verses of Scripture, allowing the Holy Spirit to take the written word and apply it as the living word in the inner being.

Campbell McAlpine

>> Choose a section of Scripture (perhaps John 15:1–17, the vine and the branches) and meditate on it for several days.

journal

101 ways to

discover

simplify

harmonize

live

enjoy God

taste

remember

explore

#48

Be Hospitable (You May Be Entertaining Ange

> *Do not forget to entertain strangers, for by so doing some people have entertained angels without knowing it.*
>
> Hebrews 13:2 NIV

hospitable

There's nothing like a good time with friends or family. As you gather in the living room, sharing laughter and stories, you can be reminded of the Supper of the Lamb when all will gather at the table and feast in the coming kingdom of God. Your friends might not be angels, but their presence in your home brings a benediction.

Practice hospitality by inviting people you don't know as well as those you do know to share your meals, especially during holidays like Thanksgiving and Christmas. You will be blessed by God and by the people you have invited into your home.

>> Invite friends to your home for a casual get-together. Invite a neighbor over for coffee.

#49

Use Your Imagination

Imagination is a God-given gift. Children use their imaginations freely, making a shoebox into a fantasy house, a broom into an airplane, and a cloud into a fairy-tale castle. Unfortunately, many adults have left their imaginations behind in childhood—and even take pride in their prosaic ways.

Use the gift of your imagination to expand your boundaries and explore your relationship with God. When you're stuck in a rut in your thinking, imagination can help you find fresh alternatives. God can speak to you through your imagination, helping you discover a different, more childlike wisdom.

imagine

Where there is no revelation, the people cast off restraint.

Proverbs 29:18
NKJV

>> The next time your thinking is stuck in a rut, try some brainstorming exercises to loosen your mental muscles.

#50

Express Love Creatively

> *It is not a matter of thinking a great deal but of loving a great deal, so do whatever arouses you most to love.*
>
> Mother Teresa

love

Love is the greatest gift you can give to someone else. When you love another person, you are essentially loving God. Look for creative ways to express your love. For example, share quiet time with a loved one. Just be together without talking, doing, making plans, or getting ready to do something else. Ask someone you love what three life wishes he or she may have. Listen intently to the answers, then meditate on ways you can help make those wishes come true.

Be creative in the ways you give love to God, too. Look for ways to make his love real in your world.

>> Try to make what is important to a loved one important to you as well. Surprise someone you love by making a date to do something together that he or she loves.

#51

Learn About the Spiritual Disciplines

The classical spiritual disciplines offer a path to a deeper inner life. Spiritual disciplines are not about dreary sackcloth and ashes, but are, rather, about becoming ever more open to the presence of God and more able to experience the highest joys of the Christian life.

Inward disciplines, such as prayer and meditation, focus on your interior life. Outward disciplines, such as simplicity and service, emphasize exterior signs of an inward grace. Corporate disciplines, such as worship and guidance, help the community celebrate God's grace. Learn more about the spiritual disciplines by reading a book.

learn

> *A small but always persistent discipline is a great force; for a soft drop falling persistently hollows out hard rock.*
>
> Isaac from Syria

>> Read *Celebration of Discipline: The Path to Spiritual Growth* by Richard Foster; it offers an excellent introduction to the spiritual disciplines.

#52

Attend a Worship Service

> *To believe God is to worship God.*
>
> Martin Luther

attend

It may be in a little white clapboard church on a country road. Or it may be in a grand cathedral in the city. There's a place of worship that will welcome you. If you don't already have a church you attend regularly, seek out a place of worship and attend a service. Whether you are a first-timer or a regular attendee, make this week's worship experience one of attentiveness and praise.

Go prepared to worship and to learn. Open your heart to receive the lessons of faith and to contribute your part to the community worship. Enjoy the time communing with God.

>> Attend a worship service at a church in your local community.

#53

Fellowship with Others

Fellowship is an old-fashioned church word packed with meaning for today's seeker. Fellowship is not only about getting together in the fellowship hall after church for tea, cookies, and a handshake. Fellowship means getting together with like-minded believers and sharing community life and worship together.

You can find heartfelt fellowship in a home Bible study, a worship service, a prayer group, or even at a retreat. You can form deep friendships in such groups. True fellowship means sharing personal triumphs and tragedies, praying for one another, and enjoying mutual encouragement.

others

> *Agree with each other, love each other, be deep-spirited friends.*
>
> Philippians 2:2
> THE MESSAGE

>> Consider opening your home to host a regular Bible study or fellowship group.

#54

Study the Bible

Make me walk along the path of your commands, for that is where my happiness is found.

Psalm 119:35 NLT

study

You can find spiritual treasure in the pages of the Bible. It is good simply to read the Bible, and you can get a lot out of it. But for deeper understanding, nothing is quite so satisfying as studying the Bible.

You can buy an all-in-one study Bible or a separate Bible handbook that offers book introductions, historical overviews, references, and guidelines for getting the most out of your study. Digging into the Bible helps you learn more about God and his ways. Your understanding will grow and you'll enjoy a deeper relationship with him.

>> Sign up for a Bible study class and enjoy the pleasures of digging into the Scripture with others.

#55

Pray an Intercessory Prayer

Intercessory prayer is a gift you give to others. It is prayer that inter-cedes—bringing the needs of another to the throne of God. This is where you help others, not merely through your own works, but by including God in the equation.

Set aside some time to pray about the needs of people you know. You may also pray for strangers you encounter on the street, for people you know in your church or community, or for needs around the world. Go to God confidently, knowing that you are offering an unseen hand of help to those in need.

pray

> *When we are linked by the power of prayer, we hold each other's hand, as it were, while we walk along a slippery path.*
>
> Saint Gregory I

>> Pray for someone in need, whether it is your hurting friend next door or someone who is suffering half a world away.

#56

Fast

> *Fasting is the voluntary denial of a normal function for the sake of intense spiritual activity.*
>
> Richard Foster

fast

Sometimes it's important to set aside a time for prayer and spiritual work. One of the spiritual disciplines that helps you nurture your spirit is fasting. When you fast for spiritual purposes, it's a private matter, not for public display. It is between you and God.

Fasting can mean going without food for a day, abstaining from certain foods for a prescribed period of time (such as giving up chocolate for Lent), or eliminating certain activities for a time (such as turning off the television for an evening to pray and read the Scriptures). Fasting helps you worship God in body as well as in spirit.

>> Use abstention from food or certain activities as an opportunity to enjoy a more intimate and focused time with God.

#57

Cast Your Anxieties on God

When you are feeling overwhelmed by life, God wants to be your comfort. Anxiety eats away at your energy and makes you less able to cope with the challenges and problems life presents. When a low-grade worry is niggling at your brain, or an unnamed fear is tugging at your emotions, it's time to take your cares to God instead of trying to carry them by yourself.

Use the simple tool of a Bible promise to help you remember the presence and help of the God who can sustain you in any difficulty. Cast your care on the one who cares for you.

anxieties

God is there, ready to help; I'm fearless no matter what. Who or what can get to me?

Hebrews 13:6
THE MESSAGE

>> Choose a promise from the Bible and personalize it. Use it as a prayer of faith when you are frightened or worried.

#58

Pray the Lord's Prayer

Your kingdom come. Your will be done on earth as it is in heaven.

Matthew 6:10 NKJV

pray

In Matthew 6:9–13, Jesus taught his disciples a prayer. Known as the Lord's Prayer, it has been prayed by the faithful for two thousand years. It has been used in corporate worship for centuries. Praying this prayer can help you delight in God and grow in grace.

This prayer offers a pattern of prayer for anyone who wishes to grow in their spiritual understanding. From difficult lessons of forgiveness to beautiful truths about trust, the Lord's Prayer offers material for personal meditation. In quiet before God or in a busy situation where you need to be reminded of God's presence, meditate on and pray this prayer.

>> Start each day this week with a heartfelt time of prayer, using the Lord's Prayer as your guide.

#59

Explore Your Faith Heritage

One of the ways you can deepen your enjoyment and understanding of God is to become more familiar with your spiritual heritage. You'll learn how others have known and enjoyed God in their own eras. You'll gain a better understanding of the faith you cherish today by learning more about the past.

Martin Luther, John Calvin, John Wesley, Saint Augustine, Saint Francis of Assisi, Origen, Saint Theresa of Avila, and Billy Graham are men and women whose lives and writings affect how you understand who God is and what he is doing in the world. Explore your own faith heritage and learn about the founders of your church.

heritage

> *What is fanaticism today is the fashionable creed tomorrow, and trite as the multiplication table a week after.*
>
> Wendell Phillips

>> Read the biography of a hero of the faith or a history of your church or denomination.

#60

Listen to the Voice of Your Heart

> *Mary treasured up all these things and pondered them in her heart.*
>
> Luke 2:19 NIV

listen

In the Christmas story, the Gospel of Luke recounts that Mary contemplated the events concerning the birth of Jesus in her heart. Paul, as told in Ephesians 1:18, prayed that "the eyes of your heart may be enlightened" (NIV).The heart is used figuratively for the hidden springs of the personal life.

Listening to your inner heart is a radical act of faith. It helps you tap into a hidden spring of life-giving spiritual wisdom. You'll discover that God whispers delightful secrets to you when you hear with your heart. When in doubt, listen to God speaking through the voice of your heart.

>> When you are facing an important decision, write a list of pros and cons. Then listen to what your heart tells you to do.

#61

Read a Children's Bible Storybook

If you are unfamiliar with the Bible, sometimes it can seem more like an impenetrable mystery than a spiritual guide. One way to remove the intimidation factor is to read a good children's Bible storybook. You can enjoy hearing Bible stories from a childlike perspective, making it easy to understand more about God.

For example, one children's book retells the story of Jonah. It's beautifully illustrated—and it shows Jonah as a mouse preaching to cats in the city of Ninevah, giving you a new understanding of why Jonah ran away. Browse the children's section and see what treasures you can discover.

read

> *Jesus prayed this prayer: "O Father, Lord of heaven and earth, thank you for hiding the truth from those who think themselves so wise and clever, and for revealing it to the childlike."*
>
> Matthew 11:25 NLT

>> The next time you are in a bookstore or a library, check out the children's book section for inspirational treasures.

#62

Trust That the Truth Will Set You Free

> *You will know the truth, and the truth will set you free.*
>
> John 8:32 NIV

trust

Jesus Christ embodied truth—showing you the reality beneath the appearance of things. When you are struggling to discern truth from illusion, listen to what God has to say about the situation or question. Let him speak to your heart, then stand in the truth you have been given.

Like Christ, choose to embody the truth, trusting that God will guide you safely through illusions and lies into the liberating truth. Let God be your safe place to stand. The God-given freedom you enjoy will make the hard places smooth, and you will delight in knowing the truth.

>> Remember a time in the past when the truth set you free. Now speak your truth and trust that you will be set free again.

#63

Ask Big Questions

ask

Many people concentrate on the small questions in life. They may be concerned about money or reputation or how to get ahead in the world. But God has a higher purpose for your life.

Instead of being defeated by old ways of looking at problems, discover the delight of asking big questions: *Why am I here? What gifts do I have to offer the world? Whom do I love and how can I love them better? What is my highest purpose in life?* When you ask these important questions, you will enjoy the big answers God wants to give you.

He who will believe only what he can fully comprehend must have a very long head or a very short creed.

Charles Caleb Colton

>> Go outside on a clear night and look up at the stars. Think about the big questions in your life in light of that awesome sky.

invite

101 ways to

imagine

share

read

worship

enjoy God

enjoy

study

pray

#64

Dance Like David Before the Lord

> David danced before the LORD with all his might, wearing a priestly tunic. So David and all Israel brought up the Ark of the LORD with much shouting and blowing of trumpets.
>
> 2 Samuel 6:14–15
> NLT

dance

It sounds stirring and exciting, doesn't it? You can almost hear the trumpets and the shouting crowd. There's David, the sweet singer of Israel and a man after God's own heart, dancing with his whole heart in joy and celebration before the ark as it makes its way up the hill and into the city. Even the critics, like David's wife, Michal, cannot dampen David's enthusiasm for celebrating God's works and wonders.

Little children dance spontaneously with joy. As a child of God, feel free to celebrate and dance like David, enjoying God with your body as well as your heart.

>> Take a dance class or explore the spiritual aspects of dance. Or just skip and clap and praise God spontaneously, like a happy child.

#65

Discover the Riches of the Bible

The Bible can help you understand who God is and how he relates to you and to all of humanity. Deepen your personal relationship with God by reading and studying the Bible.

If you are unfamiliar with the Bible, there are plenty of helps that make it accessible for the modern reader. New translations, study Bibles, Bible dictionaries and commentaries, and introductory guides can help you uncover treasures of spiritual truth in the Scriptures. You can also join a Bible study group, take a class, or listen to a taped reading of the Bible. Discover the riches of the Bible for yourself and enjoy getting to know God better.

discover

> *Divine Scripture is the feast of wisdom, and the single books are the various dishes.*
>
> Saint Ambrose

>> For a delectable dish of spiritual wisdom, pick a book of the Bible and read, study, and meditate on it for a few weeks.

#66

Shelter Your Spirit at Home

As Jesus and his disciples were on their way, he came to a village where a woman named Martha opened her home to him.

Luke 10:38 NIV

shelter

Home is where everyone goes, and most of your life takes place in your home. Whether you live alone or with a family, home is the place where the everyday and the ordinary intersect with the potential for sacred living.

From serving meals to creating beauty and order out of chaos, you can make your home a shelter for the spirit, a place where God is honored and welcomed. A home ordered around spiritual priorities frees you to enjoy time with God without distraction.

>> Plan how you can make time and space at home to honor the needs of your spirit as well as your body.

#67

Cultivate a Garden

One of the best antidotes to the hectic pace of modern life is to spend time in a garden. Whether you have a few flowerpots on the porch or a large kitchen garden, putting your hands in the earth and working with growing things offers an opportunity to pray, meditate, and dream.

As you dig up weeds, think of bad habits you want to root out of your life. As you plant seeds, remember the gifts God gave you to nurture and grow. And when the harvesttime of fruit, flower, or vegetable arrives, thank God for the bounty of blessings in your life.

cultivate

The kiss of the sun for pardon,
The song of the bird for mirth.
One is nearer God's heart in a garden
Than anywhere else on earth.

Dorothy Gurney

>> Invest in some seeds and soil (pots or plots, depending on your space) and create a garden that grows your spirit as well as plants.

#68

Bathe Your Day in Prayer

> *Perfume all your actions with the life-giving breath of prayer.*
>
> Pope John XXIII

prayer

Set aside time in the morning to bathe your day in prayer. Ask for God's presence to be with you as you take your morning shower, ferry the kids to school, make that important business appointment, eat lunch with friends, walk at the lake, shop for groceries, stop at the bank, have dinner with the family, put the dog out, let the cat in, and wind down for the evening.

Whether you live alone or with others, make God a companion in each moment. And when it's time for bed, give thanks for another day lived in the presence of God's love.

>> Start your day with prayer and set aside brief moments during the day to pray and remind yourself that God is always with you.

#69

Release Your Fear to God

Whenever you feel afraid, don't just whistle a happy tune. Take your fears and worries to God in prayer. Tell him all about it—all the details that bother you, the questions you have, the things you dread. It's easy to enjoy God when times are good, but the deepest comfort comes when you discover that God is with you in the scary times.

Now take that whole bundle of fear, worry, anxiety, and dread and release it to God. Yes, just let go and then let God take care of it. Go on with your day and trust that God will guide you in each moment as it comes.

release

> *There is no room in love for fear. Well-formed love banishes fear. Since fear is crippling, a fearful life—fear of death, fear of judgment—is one not yet fully formed in love.*
>
> 1 John 4:18
> THE MESSAGE

>> When fear makes you start feeling crazy, step back and say to yourself, "I am fine at this moment, and God is guiding me."

#70

See God in the Details

> *God is in the details.*
> Mies van der Rohe

details

When Jesus wanted to feed the five thousand, Andrew, Peter's brother, said, "Here is a boy with five small barley loaves and two small fish, but how far will they go among so many?" (John 6:9 NIV). Andrew noticed a little boy's lunch—and had no idea that God could use such a small thing to feed a great multitude.

Are there details in your life that seem unimportant in the larger scheme of things? A quick phone call, the care taken over a shared meal, or the beauty of a well-crafted sentence are all small things that God can use to his glory.

>> Look at the beauty of a well-crafted Shaker chair and think about how a simple, useful object can glorify God.

#71

Dedicate Your Work to God

Sometimes it's easy to separate your spiritual life from your work life, especially if your work isn't directly involved with a ministry or a spiritual community. But all work can be sacred, because it isn't what you do but the spirit with which you do it that makes all the difference.

If you love your work, give thanks that this is so and seek even more creative ways to serve God in it. If you are not enthusiastic about the way you earn a living, dedicate your best effort as a gift to God and ask his blessing on the work you do.

dedicate

He who labors as he prays lifts his heart to God with his hands.

Saint Bernard of Clairvaux

>> Today, no matter what happens, serve God in your daily job by looking at every customer or client as a divine appointment.

#72

Enjoy Family Devotions

The mind of Christ is to be learned in the family. Strength of character may be learned at work, but beauty of character is learned at home.

Henry Drummond

enjoy

Dad's off to work. Mom's got to ferry the kids to soccer and ballet. Brother's got football practice. Sister's in the school play. With everybody's busy schedule, it's hard to get the family together for dinner, let alone for a time of worship together.

But the rewards of family devotional time are worth the extra effort it takes to gather everyone together. Once a week, set aside a time for the entire family to get together for prayer, worship, and sharing. When you include God in your family circle, you create wonderful family memories. You'll learn to enjoy God together and grow closer as a family.

>> Set aside an hour at least once a week for prayer, spiritual reading, and gathering with family to worship God.

#73

Pray the Prayer of Relinquishment

When you want something with all your heart but you don't know when or if you'll receive it, you may need to relinquish your desire to God. When you let go and let God, you can relax, knowing that he is taking care of you.

Pray the prayer of relinquishment—entrust the desire of your heart to God. Rest in his grace and goodness. Hold on to him even when you don't understand. Leave the situation in God's hands and know that his answer will be for the highest good of all. After you've done all you can do, it is up to God to do the rest.

pray

Seek first the kingdom of God and His righteousness, and all these things shall be added to you.

Matthew 6:33
NKJV

>> Express your trust in God by going on with your daily life cheerfully and without worry or complaining.

#74

Contemplate the Love of God

> *God loves you as though you are the only person in the world, and he loves everyone the way he loves you.*
>
> Saint Augustine

love

The Bible says that God is Love. But what does this love look like to human eyes? Jesus Christ came to demonstrate the love of God and to show you the way to enjoy a reconciled relationship with God. His life shows what the Father's love is like: forgiving, compassionate, and sacrificial.

God loves you so much that he sent his Son. Meditate on the story of Christ's life, death, and resurrection. When you read his words, read them as if they are being spoken directly to you. Contemplate the love of God in Christ and how his love can transform your life.

>> Meditate on the life, death, and resurrection of Christ. Reflect on how his sacrifice expands your understanding of the meaning of divine love.

#75
Learn to Listen

A couple converse at the next table in a restaurant. The wind makes a swishing sound through the branches of a tree by your window. Cicadas sing under a summer moon. A fountain creates a trickle of cooling sound. Strains of Mozart come from an orchestra stage.

You live in a sea of sound. Whether the sounds are beautiful or unpleasant, they create a soundtrack to your life. When you train yourself to listen to life, you'll discover that you've also learned to listen to God in a new way. Let the wonder of sound teach you lessons about the wisdom of God.

listen

> *The heart of the discerning acquires knowledge; the ears of the wise seek it out.*
>
> Proverbs 18:15 NIV

>> Close your eyes and listen to the sounds that surround you. Notice how the sounds enrich your love of life and God's creation.

#76

Celebrate the Traditions of the Faith

> *Tradition is the living faith of the dead; traditionalism is the dead faith of the living.*
>
> Jaroslav Pelikan

celebrate

The traditions of the faith mark the milestones of life. Baptism signals new birth. Sabbath brings a time of rest. Communion unites God and his children. Faith traditions offer tried-and-true ways to enjoy and understand God and help make the way you live your life a reflection of his goodness.

Some traditions are for simple daily acts, like morning prayer or washing the hands before worship. Other traditions are celebrations and commemorations, such as Christmas and Easter and Lent. Appreciate the gifts passed through the generations. Learn about the traditions of your faith, and adapt some of them to your daily life.

>> Take a faith tradition, such as setting aside an entire day to celebrate Sabbath, and adapt it to your own life.

#77

Encounter God Through the Senses

senses

God gave the gifts of seeing, hearing, touching, and tasting. Yet how often are you on autopilot, so focused on what's going on in your head that you miss what's going on around you?

Creation constantly speaks to you of God. It is not a praise of words, but a form of praise that speaks in sight and sound and sensation. You are an observer of and a participant in God's work of creation. Hear God speak as you encounter today's sensational realities. Really look at a sunrise. Listen to the music of the wind. Feel the sweetness when you kiss a baby's cheek. Enjoy God.

Thank you for making me so wonderfully complex! Your workmanship is marvelous — and how well I know it.

Psalm 139:14 NLT

>> Just for today, pay attention to what reaches you through your five senses. Receive the lessons God wants to teach.

#78

Be Open to the Great Mystery

> *A religion without mystery must be a religion without God.*
>
> Jeremy Taylor

open

You live in a society that loves to reduce life to slogans and formulas. Unfortunately, people also tend to do the same with God. Yet all that anyone can understand is but a drop in the ocean compared to all there is yet to know about God. Open your heart to mystery, and worship the God who is greater than anyone can understand.

" 'I don't think the way you think. The way you work isn't the way I work.' GOD's Decree. 'For as the sky soars high above earth, so the way I work surpasses the way you work, and the way I think is beyond the way you think' " (Isaiah 55:8–9 THE MESSAGE).

>> Meditate on Isaiah 55:8–9. Think about the religious boxes you've kept God in, and open them.

#79

Pray for Peace

pray

The world is violent, divided by hate, anger, and fear. God is greater than war and terror. You can not only find comfort in his peace, but you can also become a partner with him to bring peace to the world around you.

Choose to be a peacemaker in an angry world. Pray for peace and live peacefully within yourself. Confront the emotions and attitudes that keep you from being peaceful and ask God to help you overcome them. Join with others and pray for peace on earth. Be a light of peace in your corner of the world.

> *Blessed are the peacemakers, for they shall be called sons of God.*
>
> Matthew 5:9 NKJV

>> Examine your heart and ask forgiveness for your own fear, anger, prejudice, and judgments, and then allow God's peace to fill you.

dance

101 ways to

discover

plant

bathe

release

enjoy God

dedicate

enjoy

relinquish

#80

Participate in the Community of God's People

> *The reality of our communion with Christ and in him with one another is the increase of love in our hearts.*
>
> William Temple

community

The Bible talks about being a part of the body of Christ (Ephesians 4:25). Everyone is different, yet all are one. Each person contributes to the whole to make something greater than the separate parts.

Join together with God's people and participate in the life of your faith community. Offer your gifts and talents to help others, and appreciate the unique gifts and talents others offer. You do not have to practice a Lone Ranger spirituality. Corporate worship, community service, and fellowship with people who may be wildly different but who worship the same God can be a fulfilling part of your spiritual life.

>> Join a Bible study group or a Sunday school class, or volunteer to serve on a committee.

#81

Choose to Be a Fully Alive Person

When was the last time you met someone who approached life with zest and joy? Can you remember how it felt to be in his or her presence; how that person brought a special zing that made life seem exciting and worthwhile?

Are you fully alive? Do you celebrate the life God has given you, rain or shine? Open your senses to the wonders of creation. Enjoy spending time with friends. Embrace the gifts each day brings. Be open and receptive. Choose to greet each moment with the enthusiasm of a child. Say yes to life. Saying yes to life is enjoying God at his best.

choose

The glory of God is a fully alive person.

Saint Irenaeus

>> Take a walk in the rain and enjoy getting wet. Splash in puddles like a little kid. Open your mouth and let the raindrops quench your thirst.

#82

Expand Your Circle of Love

> *Treat the foreigner the same as a native. Love him like one of your own. Remember that you were once foreigners in Egypt. I am GOD, your God.*
>
> Leviticus 19:34
> THE MESSAGE

expand

In childhood, the circle of love revolves around the family. Children grow and soon expand the circle to include new friends. Adolescents experience a larger world than smaller children, but they tend to move in cliques, eliminating those who are different from the group. In adulthood, the circle of love grows larger, yet also becomes deeper and more intimate.

As you mature spiritually, expand your circle of love. Love your friends and family, but also reach out to many other kinds of people. Love those who are different from you. The closer you grow to God, the more room you will have in your heart for others.

>> Get to know someone who comes from another city, country, or culture. Enjoy the differences and learn from them.

#83

Practice Compassion

practice

She is the waitress taking your order at the restaurant. He is the policeman who's directing traffic. She hands you a hamburger from the fast-food window. He mops the floor as you exit the building. Take the time to really see these people with compassion and empathy.

Send each person who serves you a silent prayer of blessing. See your waitress or the janitor as God's human representative. God is serving you the plate of hash browns or mopping the floors. Take delight in expressing your gratitude to God by honoring their service. Your compassionate response brings God into interactions with others.

If anyone gives even a cup of cold water to one of these little ones because he is my disciple, I tell you the truth, he will certainly not lose his reward.

Matthew 10:42 NIV

>> Be compassionate to those who serve you. Leave a generous tip for your waitress. Thank the salesclerk.

#84

Practice Forgiveness

> *He that cannot forgive others breaks the bridge over which he must pass himself; for every man has need to be forgiven.*
>
> Thomas Fuller

practice

A friend lets you down. You are the victim of a crime. Someone you trusted betrays you. You have a choice: forgive or keep holding the grudge. If you hold on to bitterness and resentment, you keep yourself hostage to the past. If you choose to practice forgiveness, you set yourself free from the past and give God room to heal the pain.

Forgiveness becomes an experience of God's grace. When you forgive others, you are more able to enjoy God's forgiveness. You know that just as you have forgiven them, even more so God has forgiven you.

>> Go to someone you have offended and ask forgiveness. Forgive someone who has hurt you.

#85

Fret Not, Fear Not

You can fritter away your energy with complaints and anxious thoughts. When you are fretful and worried, you become like a cranky child, imagining worst-case scenarios and disaster scenes around every corner.

Fear has been described as an acronym: False Expectations Appearing Real. But most of those expectations never become reality. Replace them with the energy of faith and optimism. Worry and fear are about the future, but faith is a choice you make right now. You can rest by trusting God's provision and enjoy life instead of worrying or fretting.

fear not

Don't be afraid of missing out. You're my dearest friends! The Father wants to give you the very kingdom itself.

Luke 12:32
THE MESSAGE

>> Just for today, replace every negative or fretful comment with a phrase of faith and optimism.

#86

Practice What You Preach

It does not matter whether you preach in Westminster Abbey, or teach a ragged class, so you be faithful. The faithfulness is all.

George MacDonald

practice

Do you say one thing and yet do another? Sometimes it's easier to preach it than to practice it. Yet if your life is congruent with your words, your faith becomes more meaningful and consistent. Your faithfulness glorifies God, removes the shadows of fear and condemnation, and frees you to enjoy greater intimacy with God.

When you practice what you preach, who you are and what you do become a true reflection of what you believe. Then your life becomes a joyful expression of your relationship with God.

>> Make sure your words and actions are consistent. If you say you believe God provides, then don't complain or make choices out of fear.

#87

Cultivate the Fruit of the Spirit

Virtue may not sound very glamorous. Qualities like patience and gentleness can get lost in the noise and shuffle of modern life. Yet when you meet people who are patient, kind, and loving, it doesn't matter whether they wear the latest fashions or have a big bank account. The people who exhibit the fruit of the Spirit in their lives seem to carry a bit of God's refreshing presence around with them.

Cultivating the fruit of the Spirit brings you closer to God, makes you more like him, and teaches you to take pleasure in what gives God pleasure.

cultivate

> *The Holy Spirit… will produce this kind of fruit in us: love, joy, peace, patience, kindness, goodness, faithfulness, gentleness, and self-control.*
>
> Galatians 5:22–23
> NLT

>> Think about how you can exhibit the fruit of the Spirit in your life. For example, how can you be more patient with others?

#88

Remember Those Who Have Gone Before

> *If we believe that Jesus died and rose again, even so God will bring with Him those who sleep in Jesus.*
>
> 1 Thessalonians 4:14
> NKJV

remember

You remember them for the love they gave you, the laughter and tears you shared, and the special moments that will never come again. Whether they are parents, friends, heroes, or dearly beloveds, you still miss them and wish they could be here with you again.

Remember those who have gone before, both the people you knew and the faithful saints whom you have not met. Meditate on the contributions that they made in their earthly lives. Find comfort in God's promises of eternal life and enjoy his assurance that your loved ones are safe with him now.

>> Frame a picture or make a photo collage of friends and loved ones who have passed from this life into the next.

#89

Dedicate Your Day to God

Every morning is an opportunity to start anew. When you wake up tomorrow morning, dedicate your day to God. Ask for his help and guidance throughout the day. Use a common activity, such as answering the phone or eating a meal, as a prayer reminder. For example, every time the phone rings, send a quick prayer thanking God for whatever is happening at that moment.

Just before you go to bed, think back over your day. Was it a better day than usual? Did you handle crises with more grace? Thank God for whatever happened during the day, and thank God that tomorrow offers another fresh start.

dedicate

He who gives you the day will also give you the things necessary for the day.

Gregory of Nyssa

>> Take a common activity, such as answering the phone, and use it as a reminder that today is dedicated to God.

#90
Trust in Divine Timing

> *It is not our trust that keeps us, but the God in whom we trust that keeps us.*
>
> Oswald Chambers

trust

God's timing is perfect. Sometimes it may feel late to you, but God is always on time—on divine time. When you are feeling impatient or worried, let go of your frustration and trust in divine timing.

The Scriptures use agricultural metaphors to speak about God's ways and God's timing. The field must be plowed, the seed sown, the soil watered and cultivated. Farmers do their part, but the seeds grow in their own time. It is the same in your life. You do your part. Then trust that God will work all things together in perfect order with perfect timing.

>> Plant a seed and watch it sprout, grow, and become a full-size plant. Use it as a reminder of divine timing in your life.

#91

Share Your Story

Everyone has a story to tell. Even the quietest life has its moments of heroism and triumph. Every person has struggles; every person has victories. You help others when you share your stories.

Don't be shy about sharing your story when the opportunity arises. You have something special to offer. Others will be encouraged by your experiences. They will be blessed by what you've learned and the things God has done in your life. Even your failures and short-comings are an important part of the story. Telling stories to one another is a way to praise God for all he has done.

share

> To be a witness does not consist of engaging in propaganda or in stirring people up. It means to live in such a way that one's life would not make sense if God did not exist.
>
> Emmanuel Suhard

>> Get together with a friend and tell each other stories of your lives and how God has been faithful through it all.

#92

Let Children Be Your Teachers

Mark this: Unless you accept God's kingdom in the simplicity of a child, you'll never get in.

Mark 10:15
THE MESSAGE

teachers

When the disciples tried to shoo the children away, Jesus told them to let the little children come to him. He told them that they should be like children, and that a child's heart receives the kingdom of God.

If you've been around sophisticated and jaded adults too much lately, take a time-out on the playground. Spend a little time with children and let them teach you. Sit down and ask a child about dreams, wonder, and God. Watch children explore the world and experience life. Then you'll learn something about enjoying God.

>> Spend time with children. Learn from them and let them remind you of a more innocent faith that is based in wonder.

#93

Relax and Enjoy the Journey

"Are we there yet?" the children ask on a family vacation. "Are we there yet?" you ask God when you are working toward a cherished goal. Sit back and enjoy the process. Appreciate the view. Enjoy the stops along the way. There is as much joy in the journey as the destination for those who know how to relax and trust God.

God leads you step by step along the path. Sometimes you may not know where that path is taking you. But with God beside you, the journey can be sweet, even in difficult times. You'll miss the blessings of the journey if you're focused on only the destination.

relax

You've got my feet on the life path, all radiant from the shining of your face. Ever since you took my hand, I'm on the right way.

Psalm 16:11
THE MESSAGE

>> Take a drive in the country. Enjoy the journey by stopping at vegetable stands, historical markers, or viewpoints along the way.

#94

Make a Decision to Follow God

> We make our decisions, and then our decisions turn around and make us.
>
> Francis Willliam Boreham

follow

If you have felt far away from God lately, renew your commitment to following him. Make a decision that can change your life profoundly: the decision to seek after God and follow where he takes you.

When you choose to follow God, with no holding back and no reservations, get ready for some wonderful changes. Old habits and companions may fall away. New pleasures and friends will enter your life. Attitudes will shift; priorities will change. When God is at the center of your heart, then the rest of your life will order itself around him. It's the best decision you'll ever make.

>> Mark this date in your journal or calendar as the day you decided to follow God with all your heart.

#95

Practice Art as Meditation

Slosh some paint on canvas or paper. Put your fingers in a mound of clay and make a pot. Make a collage of pictures from old magazines. Doing creative work as an active form of meditation can be healing and enlightening.

Practicing art as meditation can help you express yourself, understand yourself better, and contemplate the world around you. Over the centuries, art has also been a vehicle for meditating on God. Great paintings and sculptures and mosaics have been created to praise God, to aid in worship, and to express the imaginative spirit that reflects the Creator.

practice

Every artist dips his brush in his own soul, and paints his own nature into his pictures.

Henry Ward Beecher

>> Collect twenty images that reflect your life or interests. Create a collage with them. What does your collage tell you about yourself?

participate

101 ways to

choose

expand

forgive

practice

enjoy God

trust

let go

receive

#96

Welcome the Unknown

> *Trust the past to God's mercy, the present to God's love, and the future to God's providence.*
>
> Saint Augustine

unknown

Predictability is prized in a society that runs on flow charts, demographic studies, and marketing plans. You have been taught to punch out a product, project your earnings, and make accurate predictions about what will happen tomorrow and what you'll do.

But life is much larger than the charts and graphs and plans that are made. James 4:14 says that people do not know what will happen tomorrow. But God knows. A faithful God holds you, so you can hold life lightly. Instead of trying to predict and control everything, welcome the unknown. You can do this because you trust a mighty God.

>> Do something you've never done before or go someplace you've never been. Enjoy experiencing something new.

#97
Enter into Grace

Theologians have debated the meaning of *grace* for centuries. Grace is a gift of God that brings humanity into the mercy, freedom, and love of God. John Newton, the former slave trader, wrote the hymn "Amazing Grace," saying, " 'Tis grace that brought me safe thus far, and grace will lead me home."

Grace is larger than any theology or dogma. It is an expression of the love and mercy of God. Grace is God's answer to your cry for help. He gives his forgiveness freely through Christ. Enter into God's grace, trust in divine mercy, and accept the love that answered before you called.

g r a c e

> *No one is safe by his own strength, but he is safe by the grace and mercy of God.*
>
> Cyprian

>> Look in the mirror and see yourself as someone God loves.

#98

Live Your Life from the Heart

> *I would rather make mistakes in kindness and compassion than work miracles in unkindness and hardness.*
>
> Mother Teresa

heart

The marketing mind loves to buy and sell. It lives in the head, valuing people for what they can produce or how much they will buy. The heart knows a different way of being that money, productivity, or material success cannot measure.

If you want to live a Christlike life, live it from the heart. The heart values courage, beauty, creativity, and love. The heart knows that all the material success in the world is meaningless without love. Value people because God loves them. Make love a priority in your life, and treasure the values of the heart.

>> Send five postcards to people you love. Tell them how much you love them.

#99

Delight in Creativity

Creativity is your birthright. Like the Creator God, you are a creator. You can express your creativity with paint, clay, music, or drama. But you can also express your creativity through building a business, making your home beautiful, planting a garden, or making a delicious meal.

Delight in creativity. Learn new skills. Discover new ways of doing things. Enjoy the materials of creation and express yourself with them. Enjoy making and doing things. God created you in his image. Reflect that image back to God by expressing your creativity.

creativity

God loves material things. He made them!

C. S. Lewis

>> Spend time working on a favorite creative project. Visit an art exhibit, a museum, or a crafts store for inspiration.

#100

Celebrate Your Victories

These things I remember as I pour out my soul: how I used to go with the multitude, leading the procession to the house of God, with shouts of joy and thanksgiving among the festive throng.

Psalm 42:4 NIV

celebrate

When God has done something wonderful in your life, savor the victory. Celebrate, just as the children of Israel did after the Red Sea parted and they escaped from the Egyptians. Every victory, great or small, can be an opportunity to celebrate what God has done in your life.

If you have experienced a healing—a spontaneous miracle, or the miracle of a body doing its natural job of mending—praise God. If you were protected in an accident or if money came in to pay an unexpected bill or if you've just rediscovered the joy of your salvation, celebrate your victory and praise God.

>> Call a friend or loved one to share your victory or answered prayer. Get together for a victory celebration.

#101

Let God Have the Last Word

When you want to prove that you are right, or when you want to defend a pet opinion or belief, let go of your bull-dog tenacity and let God have the last word. Whether your argument is with human beings or with God, in the end only God is wise enough to know all the answers.

Let go of your need to be approved in the eyes of others, and of the temptation to always have the last word in any conversation. Relax into God's approval instead of being afraid of what others think. Depend on his wisdom instead of on your own wisdom.

word

I'm A to Z, the First and the Final, Beginning and Conclusion.

Revelation 22:13
THE MESSAGE

>> The next time you are trying to prove yourself, stop arguing. Let God make the final judgment, let him have the last word.

God loves you as though you are the only person in the world,
and he loves everyone the way he loves you.

Saint Augustine

Seek first the kingdom of God and His righteousness, and all these things shall be added to you.

Matthew 6:33 NKJV